MILE by MILE

by
S. N. PIKE, M.B.E.

KINGS CROSS EDITION
L.N.E.R.

The journey between London and the North described detail:—

- ● GRADIENTS OF THE LINE

- ● SPEED TESTS AND MILEAGES

- ● VIADUCTS, BRIDGES AND EMBANKMENTS

- ● TUNNELS, CUTTINGS AND CROSSOVERS

- ● STREAMS, RIVERS AND ROADS

- ● TOWNS, VILLAGES AND CHURCHES

- ● MINES, FACTORIES AND WORKS

with an account of features of interest and beauty to be seen from the train.

A facsimile reprint by

Silver Link Publishing Ltd
Unit 5, Home Farm Close, Church Street,
Wadenhoe, Peterborough PE8 5TE

Originally published in 1947 by Atlas Publishing Company
Facsimile edition first published in December 1988
by Silver Link Publishing Ltd
Reprinted March 1993

British Library Cataloguing in Publication Data

Pike, S. N. (Stuart N)
Mile by mile on the LNER. – Kings Cross edition
I. Title
385.0941

ISBN 0 947971 89 0

Printed and bound in Great Britain

ERRATA

Map 14 (Page 16) : *The true position of mileposts 165, 166 and 167 is slightly north of where indicated on this map, milepost 167 being north of the Goole Canal, not south of the bridge as shown.*

Map 16 (Page 18) : *The correct name of the Junction 2 miles north of York is Skelton Junct., not Poppleton as shown.*

Author's Note

The pleasures and thrills of the journey between Kings Cross and Edinburgh are limitless. Every mile of the trip embraces some special feature of interest or beauty to compel the attention of the passenger.

The object of this little book is to encourage the passenger to anticipate his progress, and to enable him to know, to a nicety, what he next will see from the window at any and every stage of the journey. It is such a pity to sacrifice this experience to idle slumber, or to concentration on a magazine that would the better be enjoyed at home.

The beautiful countryside rushes by; beneath the tranquil surface, right beside the line, miners are toiling for the black diamonds essential to feed the great industrial plants we pass.

I acknowledge, with grateful thanks, certain information given me by Officials of the L.N.E.R. Railwaymen of every grade have contributed their share to make this publication as complete as possible. Railwaymen are justly proud of the vast organisation they serve; it is their wish that passengers should enjoy to the full the journeys they make with such speed and safety. The information and advice they have so readily placed at my disposal has been gladly offered with that end in view.

Shepperton, 1947.   S. N. P.

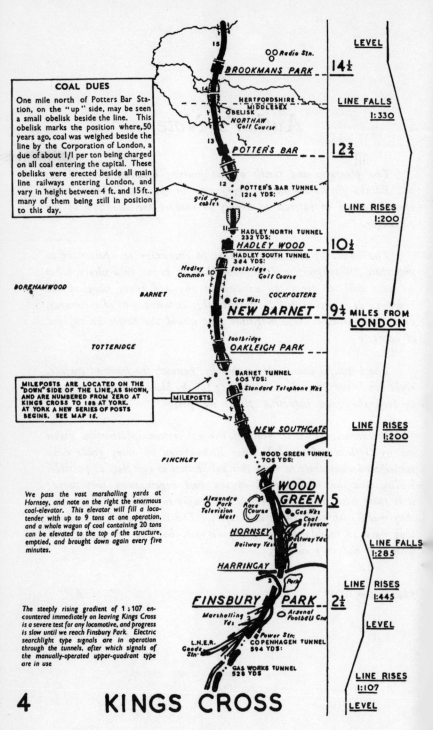

LEVEL

14½

BROOKMANS PARK

⊙⊙ *Radio Stn.*

LINE FALLS
1:330

COAL DUES

One mile north of Potters Bar Station, on the "up" side, may be seen a small obelisk beside the line. This obelisk marks the position where, 50 years ago, coal was weighed beside the line by the Corporation of London, a due of about 1/1 per ton being charged on all coal entering the capital. These obelisks were erected beside all main line railways entering London, and vary in height between 4 ft. and 15 ft., many of them being still in position to this day.

HERTFORDSHIRE
MIDDLESEX

OBELISK

NORTHAW
Golf Course

POTTER'S BAR

12¾

14

13

12

POTTER'S BAR TUNNEL
1214 YDS.

grid cables

LINE RISES
1:200

11

HADLEY NORTH TUNNEL
232 YDS.

HADLEY WOOD

10½

HADLEY SOUTH TUNNEL
384 YDS.

Hadley Common

10

footbridge

Golf Course

BOREHAMWOOD

BARNET

COCKFOSTERS

⊙ *Gas Wks.*

NEW BARNET

9¾ MILES FROM
LONDON

TOTTERIDGE

footbridge

OAKLEIGH PARK

MILEPOSTS ARE LOCATED ON THE "DOWN" SIDE OF THE LINE, AS SHOWN, AND ARE NUMBERED FROM ZERO AT KINGS CROSS TO 188 AT YORK. AT YORK A NEW SERIES OF POSTS BEGINS. SEE MAP 16.

MILEPOSTS

8

BARNET TUNNEL
605 YDS.

Standard Telephone Wks

7

NEW SOUTHGATE

LINE RISES
1:200

FINCHLEY

WOOD GREEN TUNNEL
705 YDS.

WOOD GREEN

5

We pass the vast marshalling yards at Hornsey, and note on the right the enormous coal-elevator. This elevator will fill a loco-tender with up to 9 tons at one operation, and a whole wagon of coal containing 20 tons can be elevated to the top of the structure, emptied, and brought down again every five minutes.

*Alexandra
Park
Television
Mast*

*Race
Course*

⊙ *Gas Wks.
Coal
elevator*

HORNSEY

Railway Yds.

Railway Yds.

LINE FALLS
1:285

HARRINGAY

3

Park

LINE RISES
1:445

FINSBURY PARK

2½

*Marshalling
Yds.*

⊙ *Arsenal
Football Gnd.*

LEVEL

The steeply rising gradient of 1:107 encountered immediately on leaving Kings Cross is a severe test for any locomotive, and progress is slow until we reach Finsbury Park. Electric searchlight type signals are in operation through the tunnels, after which signals of the manually-operated upper-quadrant type are in use

L.N.E.R.
Goods
Stn.

⊙ *Power Stn.*
COPENHAGEN TUNNEL
594 YDS.

LINE RISES
1:107

GAS WORKS TUNNEL
528 YDS.

4

KINGS CROSS

LEVEL

LONDON—EDINBURGH

EXACT DISTANCES BETWEEN STATIONS—EXPRESS TRAIN RUNNING·TIMES

(1) STATION	(2) Distance Between Stations		(3) Express Train Running Times	(4) Actual Running Times			(5) NOTES and Average Speeds over each Section
	Miles	Yards	Minutes	Minutes	Early	Late	
KING'S CROSS to HATFIELD	17	1,199	27				From a standing start the heavily laden express encounters a severe 1 : 107 gradient through the Gasworks and Copenhagen tunnels, to be followed by a steep 1 : 200 climb for 8 miles from milepost 4 to Poters Bar, where the summit is reached. From here we rush through Hatfield at really high speed. Average speed 39.0 m.p.h., the low figure being due to the difficult start. (See Maps 4 and 5.)
HATFIELD to HITCHIN	14	424	14				The summit on this section is at Woolmer Green Box, near milepost 24. The junction of the lines at Langley are passed at 65 to 70 m.p.h. Water is taken on at the Troughs at milepost 27 at this speed, which we maintain through Hitchin. Average speed 61 m.p.h. (See Maps 5 and 6.)
HITCHIN to HUNTINGDON	26	1,672	26				This is a really fast section of the line, and, except for a slowing down for curves near Offord, a very high speed is maintained. Average speed 62.3 m.p.h. (See Maps 6 and 7.)
HUNTINGDON to PETERBOROUGH	17	863	19				An exceptionally fast section of the line. The necessity for approaching Peterborough at a minimum pace reduces our average speed to 55.2 m.p.h. (See Maps 7 and 8.)
PETERBOROUGH to GRANTHAM	29	165	44				From a standing start at Peterborough we encounter a series of rising gradients from milepost 85 for the next 15 miles. Over the summit we pass through Great Ponton at very high speed, slowing down slightly for Grantham. Average speed 39.5 m.p.h. (See Maps 8, 9 and 10.)
GRANTHAM to NEWARK	14	1,138	14				Very high speeds are attained on the falling gradients. Average over the section 63.2 m.p.h. (See Maps 10 and 11.)
NEWARK to RETFORD	18	902	24				Between Newark and milepost 128 the line is dead level, but rising gradients up to Askham tunnel lower the average. Speed is sharply reduced approaching Retford. Average speed 46.2 m.p.h. (See Maps 12 and 13.)

(Continued on page 13)

5

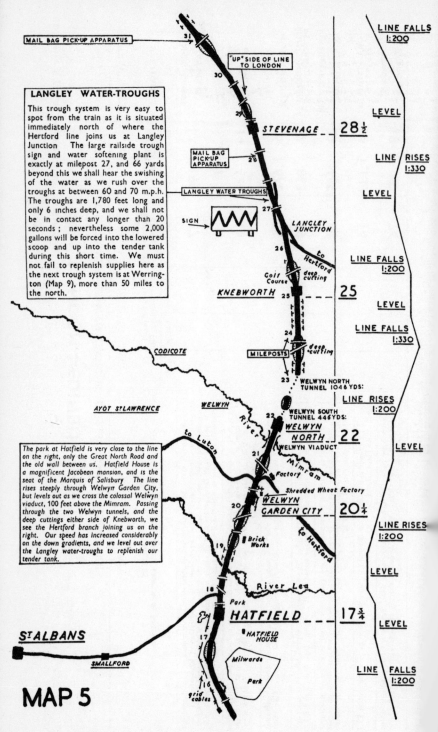

MAIL BAG PICK-UP APPARATUS

"UP" SIDE OF LINE TO LONDON

LANGLEY WATER-TROUGHS

This trough system is very easy to spot from the train as it is situated immediately north of where the Hertford line joins us at Langley Junction The large railside trough sign and water softening plant is exactly at milepost 27, and 66 yards beyond this we shall hear the swishing of the water as we rush over the troughs at between 60 and 70 m.p.h. The troughs are 1,780 feet long and only 6 inches deep, and we shall not be in contact any longer than 20 seconds ; nevertheless some 2,000 gallons will be forced into the lowered scoop and up into the tender tank during this short time. We must not fail to replenish supplies here as the next trough system is at Werrington (Map 9), more than 50 miles to the north.

MAIL BAG PICK-UP APPARATUS

LANGLEY WATER TROUGHS

SIGN

STEVENAGE

LANGLEY JUNCTION

to Hertford

CODICOTE

Golf Course

deep cutting

KNEBWORTH

MILEPOSTS

deep cutting

AYOT St LAWRENCE

WELWYN

River

WELWYN NORTH TUNNEL 1046 YDS:

WELWYN SOUTH TUNNEL 446 YDS:

to Luton

WELWYN NORTH

WELWYN VIADUCT

Mimram

The park at Hatfield is very close to the line on the right, only the Great North Road and the old wall between us. Hatfield House is a magnificent Jacobean mansion, and is the seat of the Marquis of Salisbury The line rises steeply through Welwyn Garden City, but levels out as we cross the colossal Welwyn viaduct, 100 feet above the Mimram. Passing through the two Welwyn tunnels, and the deep cuttings either side of Knebworth, we see the Hertford branch joining us on the right. Our speed has increased considerably on the down gradients, and we level out over the Langley water-troughs to replenish our tender tank.

Factory

Shredded Wheat Factory

WELWYN GARDEN CITY

to Hertford

Brick Works

River Lea

Park

HATFIELD

HATFIELD HOUSE

St ALBANS

SMALLFORD

Milwards Park

grid cables

MAP 5

Gradient profile (right side)

LINE FALLS 1:200

LEVEL — 28½

LINE RISES 1:330

LEVEL

LINE FALLS 1:200

LEVEL — 25

LINE FALLS 1:330

LINE RISES 1:200

LEVEL — 22

LEVEL — 20¼

LINE RISES 1:200

LEVEL

LEVEL — 17¾

LEVEL

LINE FALLS 1:200

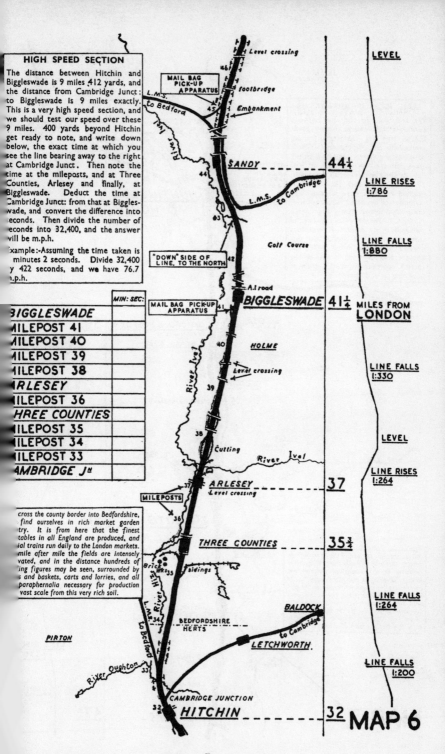

HIGH SPEED SECTION

The distance between Hitchin and Biggleswade is 9 miles 412 yards, and the distance from Cambridge Junct: to Biggleswade is 9 miles exactly. This is a very high speed section, and we should test our speed over these 9 miles. 400 yards beyond Hitchin get ready to note, and write down below, the exact time at which you see the line bearing away to the right at Cambridge Junct. Then note the time at the mileposts, and at Three Counties, Arlesey and finally, at Biggleswade. Deduct the time at Cambridge Junct: from that at Biggleswade, and convert the difference into seconds. Then divide the number of seconds into 32,400, and the answer will be m.p.h.

Example:—Assuming the time taken is 7 minutes 2 seconds. Divide 32,400 by 422 seconds, and we have 76.7 m.p.h.

	MIN: SEC:
BIGGLESWADE	
MILEPOST 41	
MILEPOST 40	
MILEPOST 39	
MILEPOST 38	
ARLESEY	
MILEPOST 36	
THREE COUNTIES	
MILEPOST 35	
MILEPOST 34	
MILEPOST 33	
CAMBRIDGE Jn	

cross the county border into Bedfordshire, find ourselves in rich market garden try. It is from here that the finest tables in all England are produced, and ial trains run daily to the London markets. mile after mile the fields are intensely vated, and in the distance hundreds of ing figures may be seen, surrounded by s and baskets, carts and lorries, and all paraphernalia necessary for production vast scale from this very rich soil.

Level crossing
footbridge
Embankment
MAIL BAG PICK-UP APPARATUS
L.M.S. to Bedford
SANDY
L.M.S. to Cambridge
Golf Course
"DOWN" SIDE OF LINE, TO THE NORTH
A.1 road
MAIL BAG PICK-UP APPARATUS
BIGGLESWADE
HOLME
Level crossing
River Ivel
Cutting
River Ivel
MILEPOSTS
ARLESEY
Level crossing
THREE COUNTIES
River Hitchin
Br dings
BEDFORDSHIRE HERTS
BALDOCK
to Cambridge
LETCHWORTH
PIRTON
River Oughton
L.M.S. to Bedford
CAMBRIDGE JUNCTION
HITCHIN

LEVEL

44¼

LINE RISES 1:786

LINE FALLS 1:880

41¼ MILES FROM LONDON

LINE FALLS 1:330

LEVEL

LINE RISES 1:264

37

35¾

LINE FALLS 1:264

LINE FALLS 1:200

32 MAP 6

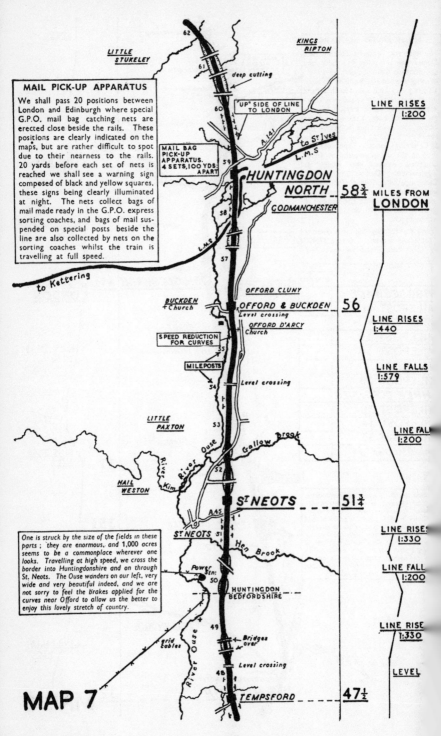

LITTLE
STUKELEY

KINGS
RIPTON

62

61

deep cutting

60

"UP" SIDE OF LINE
TO LONDON

A.141

to St Ives
L.M.S

MAIL PICK-UP APPARATUS

We shall pass 20 positions between London and Edinburgh where special G.P.O. mail bag catching nets are erected close beside the rails. These positions are clearly indicated on the maps, but are rather difficult to spot due to their nearness to the rails. 20 yards before each set of nets is reached we shall see a warning sign composed of black and yellow squares, these signs being clearly illuminated at night. The nets collect bags of mail made ready in the G.P.O. express sorting coaches, and bags of mail suspended on special posts beside the line are also collected by nets on the sorting coaches whilst the train is travelling at full speed.

MAIL BAG
PICK-UP
APPARATUS.
4 SETS, 100 YDS.
APART

59

**HUNTINGDON
NORTH** — 58¾

GODMANCHESTER

58

L.M.S

57

to Kettering

OFFORD CLUNY

OFFORD & BUCKDEN — 56

BUCKDEN
+ Church

Level crossing

OFFORD D'ARCY
Church

SPEED REDUCTION
FOR CURVES

55

MILEPOSTS

54

Level crossing

LITTLE
PAXTON

53

Gallow Brook

River Ouse

52

River Kim

HAIL
WESTON

St NEOTS — 51¾

A.45

St NEOTS

51

Hen Brook

One is struck by the size of the fields in these parts; they are enormous, and 1,000 acres seems to be a commonplace wherever one looks. Travelling at high speed, we cross the border into Huntingdonshire and on through St. Neots. The Ouse wanders on our left, very wide and very beautiful indeed, and we are not sorry to feel the brakes applied for the curves near Offord to allow us the better to enjoy this lovely stretch of country.

Power
Stn:
50

HUNTINGDON
BEDFORDSHIRE

49

grid
cables

River Ouse

Bridges
over

Level crossing

48

MAP 7

TEMPSFORD — 47½

LINE RISES
1:200

MILES FROM
LONDON

LINE RISES
1:440

LINE FALLS
1:579

LINE FALL
1:200

LINE RISES
1:330

LINE FALL
1:200

LINE RISE
1:330

LEVEL

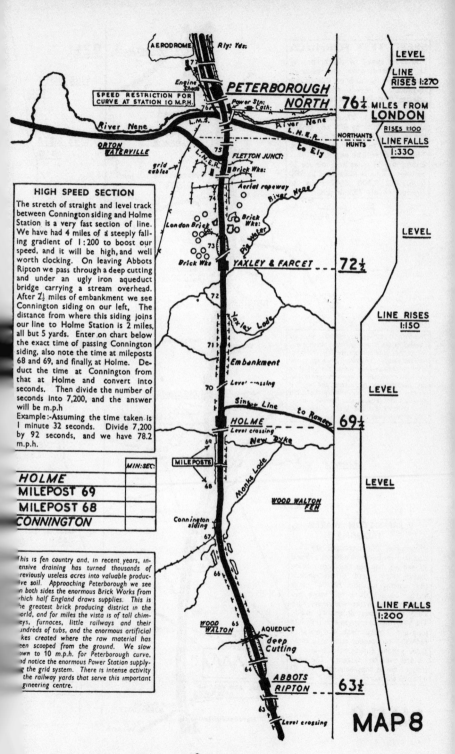

AERODROME   Rly: Yds:

SPEED RESTRICTION FOR
CURVE AT STATION 10 M.P.H.

Engine Sheds

PETERBOROUGH
Power Stn: Cath: **NORTH**

76¼ MILES FROM
LONDON

River Nene   River Nene
L.M.S.   L.N.E.R.   To Ely

ORTON WATERVILLE   NORTHANTS
HUNTS

grid cables   L.N.E.R.   FLETTON JUNCT:

Brick Wks:

Aerial ropeway   River Nene

London Brick   Brick Wks:

Pig Water   **YAXLEY & FARCET**   72½

Brick Wks   Yaxley Lode

Embankment

Level crossing

Sink's Line   to Ramsey   69½

HOLME
Level crossing

New Dyke

MILEPOSTS   Monks Lode

WOOD WALTON FEN

Connington siding

This is fen country and, in recent years, intensive draining has turned thousands of
previously useless acres into valuable produc-
tive soil. Approaching Peterborough we see
on both sides the enormous Brick Works from
which half England draws supplies. This is
the greatest brick producing district in the
world, and for miles the vista is of tall chim-
neys, furnaces, little railways and their
hundreds of tubs, and the enormous artificial
lakes created where the raw material has
been scooped from the ground. We slow
down to 10 m.p.h. for Peterborough curve,
and notice the enormous Power Station supply-
ing the grid system. There is intense activity
in the railway yards that serve this important
engineering centre.

WOOD WALTON   AQUEDUCT

deep Cutting

ABBOTS RIPTON   63½

Level crossing

MAP 8

HIGH SPEED SECTION

The stretch of straight and level track
between Connington siding and Holme
Station is a very fast section of line.
We have had 4 miles of a steeply falling gradient of 1:200 to boost our
speed, and it will be high, and well
worth clocking. On leaving Abbots
Ripton we pass through a deep cutting
and under an ugly iron aqueduct
bridge carrying a stream overhead.
After 2½ miles of embankment we see
Connington siding on our left. The
distance from where this siding joins
our line to Holme Station is 2 miles,
all but 5 yards. Enter on chart below
the exact time of passing Connington
siding, also note the time at mileposts
68 and 69, and finally, at Holme. Deduct the time at Connington from
that at Holme and convert into
seconds. Then divide the number of
seconds into 7,200, and the answer
will be m.p.h
Example:-Assuming the time taken is
1 minute 32 seconds. Divide 7,200
by 92 seconds, and we have 78.2
m.p.h.

	MIN:SEC:
HOLME	
MILEPOST 69	
MILEPOST 68	
CONNINGTON	

LEVEL

LINE RISES 1:270

RISES 1:100

LINE FALLS 1:330

LEVEL

LINE RISES 1:150

LEVEL

LEVEL

LINE FALLS 1:200

9

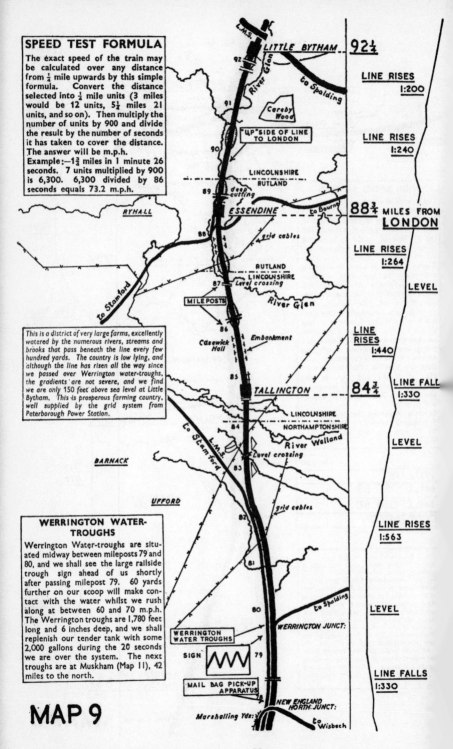

SPEED TEST FORMULA

The exact speed of the train may be calculated over any distance from $\frac{1}{4}$ mile upwards by this simple formula. Convert the distance selected into $\frac{1}{4}$ mile units (3 miles would be 12 units, $5\frac{1}{4}$ miles 21 units, and so on). Then multiply the number of units by 900 and divide the result by the number of seconds it has taken to cover the distance. The answer will be m.p.h.

Example:—$1\frac{3}{4}$ miles in 1 minute 26 seconds. 7 units multiplied by 900 is 6,300. 6,300 divided by 86 seconds equals 73.2 m.p.h.

This is a district of very large farms, excellently watered by the numerous rivers, streams and brooks that pass beneath the line every few hundred yards. The country is low lying, and although the line has risen all the way since we passed over Werrington water-troughs, the gradients are not severe, and we find we are only 150 feet above sea level at Little Bytham. This is prosperous farming country, well supplied by the grid system from Peterborough Power Station.

WERRINGTON WATER-TROUGHS

Werrington Water-troughs are situated midway between mileposts 79 and 80, and we shall see the large railside trough sign ahead of us shortly after passing milepost 79. 60 yards further on our scoop will make contact with the water whilst we rush along at between 60 and 70 m.p.h. The Werrington troughs are 1,780 feet long and 6 inches deep, and we shall replenish our tender tank with some 2,000 gallons during the 20 seconds we are over the system. The next troughs are at Muskham (Map 11), 42 miles to the north.

LITTLE BYTHAM — **92¼**

LINE RISES 1:200

LINE RISES 1:240

88¾ MILES FROM **LONDON**

LINE RISES 1:264

LEVEL

LINE RISES 1:440

84¾

LINE FALL 1:330

LEVEL

LINE RISES 1:563

LEVEL

LINE FALLS 1:330

L.M.S.

River Glen

Careby Wood

"UP" SIDE OF LINE TO LONDON

LINCOLNSHIRE RUTLAND

deep cutting

to Bourne

ESSENDINE

RYHALL

grid cables

to Stamford

RUTLAND LINCOLNSHIRE
Level crossing

River Glen

MILE POSTS

Casewick Hall

Embankment

TALLINGTON

LINCOLNSHIRE NORTHAMPTONSHIRE

River Welland

to Stamford

L.M.S.
Level crossing

BARNACK

UFFORD

grid cables

to Spalding

WERRINGTON WATER TROUGHS

SIGN

WERRINGTON JUNCT:

MAIL BAG PICK-UP APPARATUS

NEW ENGLAND NORTH. JUNCT:

Marshalling Yds:

to Wisbech

MAP 9

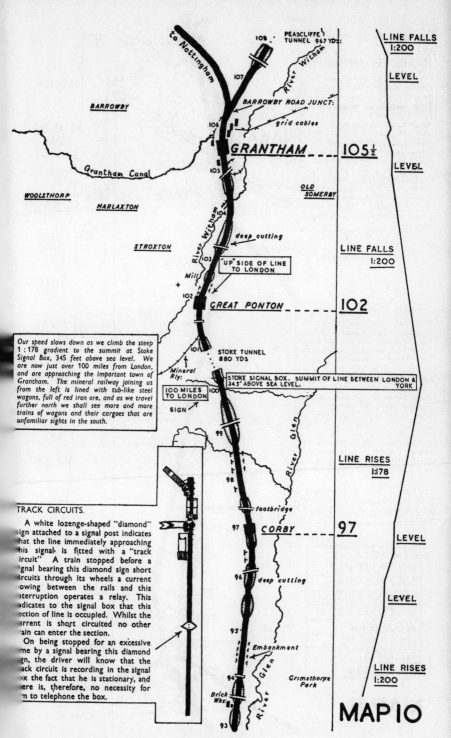

to Nottingham

BARROWBY

Grantham Canal

WOOLSTHORP

HARLAXTON

STROXTON

Mill

108

107

Peascliffe Tunnel 967 YDS.

River Witham

BARROWBY ROAD JUNCT:

grid cables

106

GRANTHAM — — **105½**

105

OLD SOMERBY

104

River Witham

deep cutting

103

UP SIDE OF LINE TO LONDON

102

GREAT PONTON — — **102**

101

STOKE TUNNEL 880 YDS

Mineral Rly:

STOKE SIGNAL BOX. SUMMIT OF LINE BETWEEN LONDON & YORK 345' ABOVE SEA LEVEL.

100 MILES TO LONDON SIGN

100

99

98

footbridge

97 **CORBY** — — **97**

96 deep cutting

95

Embankment

94

Brick Wks

93

River Glen

River Glen

Grimsthorpe Park

LINE FALLS 1:200

LEVEL

LEVEL

LINE FALLS 1:200

LINE RISES 1:178

LEVEL

LEVEL

LINE RISES 1:200

MAP 10

Our speed slows down as we climb the steep 1 : 178 gradient to the summit at Stoke Signal Box, 345 feet above sea level. We are now just over 100 miles from London, and are approaching the important town of Grantham. The mineral railway joining us from the left is lined with tub-like steel wagons, full of red iron ore, and as we travel further north we shall see more and more trains of wagons and their cargoes that are unfamiliar sights in the south.

TRACK CIRCUITS.

A white lozenge-shaped "diamond" sign attached to a signal post indicates that the line immediately approaching this signal is fitted with a "track circuit." A train stopped before a signal bearing this diamond sign short circuits through its wheels a current flowing between the rails and this interruption operates a relay. This indicates to the signal box that this section of line is occupied. Whilst the current is short circuited no other train can enter the section.

On being stopped for an excessive time by a signal bearing this diamond sign, the driver will know that the track circuit is recording in the signal box the fact that he is stationary, and there is, therefore, no necessity for him to telephone the box.

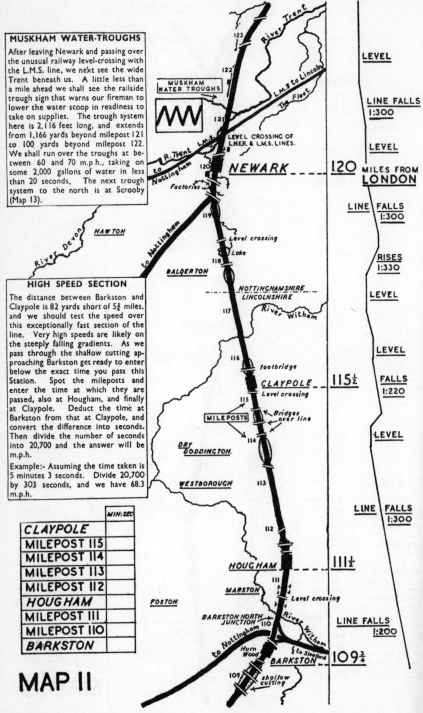

MUSKHAM WATER-TROUGHS

After leaving Newark and passing over the unusual railway level-crossing with the L.M.S. line, we next see the wide Trent beneath us. A little less than a mile ahead we shall see the railside trough sign that warns our fireman to lower the water scoop in readiness to take on supplies. The trough system here is 2,116 feet long, and extends from 1,166 yards beyond milepost 121 to 100 yards beyond milepost 122. We shall run over the troughs at between 60 and 70 m.p.h., taking on some 2,000 gallons of water in less than 20 seconds. The next trough system to the north is at Scrooby (Map 13).

HIGH SPEED SECTION

The distance between Barkston and Claypole is 82 yards short of 5¾ miles, and we should test the speed over this exceptionally fast section of the line. Very high speeds are likely on the steeply falling gradients. As we pass through the shallow cutting approaching Barkston get ready to enter below the exact time you pass this Station. Spot the mileposts and enter the time at which they are passed, also at Hougham, and finally at Claypole. Deduct the time at Barkston from that at Claypole, and convert the difference into seconds. Then divide the number of seconds into 20,700 and the answer will be m.p.h.

Example:- Assuming the time taken is 5 minutes 3 seconds. Divide 20,700 by 303 seconds, and we have 68.3 m.p.h.

	MIN: SEC
CLAYPOLE	
MILEPOST 115	
MILEPOST 114	
MILEPOST 113	
MILEPOST 112	
HOUGHAM	
MILEPOST 111	
MILEPOST 110	
BARKSTON	

MAP 11

MUSKHAM
WATER TROUGHS →

LEVEL CROSSING OF
L.N.E.R. & L.M.S. LINES.

NEWARK

Factories

HAWTON

River Devon

BALDERTON

NOTTINGHAMSHIRE
LINCOLNSHIRE

River Witham

Level crossing

Lake

footbridge

CLAYPOLE
Level crossing

MILEPOSTS

Bridges over line

DRY DODDINGTON.

WESTBOROUGH

HOUGHAM

MARSTON

FOSTON

Level crossing

BARKSTON NORTH
JUNCTION

to Nottingham

Hurn Wood

to Sleaford

BARKSTON

shallow cutting

to Nottingham

River Trent

River Trent L.M.S.

L.M.S. to Lincoln

The Fleet

123

122

121

120

119

118

117

116

115

114

113

112

111

110

109

River Witham

LEVEL
LINE FALLS 1:300
LEVEL
120 MILES FROM LONDON
LINE FALLS 1:300
RISES 1:330
LEVEL
LEVEL
115½ FALLS 1:220
LEVEL
LINE FALLS 1:300
111½
LINE FALLS 1:200
109¾

12

LONDON—EDINBURGH

EXACT DISTANCES BETWEEN STATIONS—EXPRESS TRAIN RUNNING TIMES

(1) STATION	(2) Distance Between Stations		(3) Express Train Running Times	(4) Actual Running Times			(5) NOTES and Average Speeds over each Section
	Miles	Yards	Minutes	Minutes	Early	Late	
RETFORD to DONCASTER	17	611	19				Falling gradients approaching Scrooby water-troughs send us over the water pick-up at 65 m.p.h. The line rises steeply to milepost 150, but we again make fine speed to the outskirts of Doncaster. Average speed 55.2 m.p.h. (See Maps 12 and 13.)
DONCASTER to YORK	32	308	42				The 6 miles of level track between mileposts 158 and 166 is a high speed section, and well worth "clocking." We slow down for the curve and swing bridge at Selby and also for the curve at Chaloner's Whin Junction. The sharp curve at York is approached slowly. Average speed 46.0 m.p.h. (See Maps 14, 15 and 16.)
YORK to THIRSK	22	352	25				12 miles of dead level and dead straight track allows for really fast travelling. By the time we reach Tollerton, speeds are in excess of 75 m.p.h. The standing start at York, however, reduces our average to 53.4 m.p.h. (See Maps 16 and 17.)
THIRSK to NORTHALLERTON	7	1,320	8				The line rises very slightly. This section is covered at an average of 58.1 m.p.h. (See Maps 17 and 18.)
NORTHALLERTON to DARLINGTON	14	308	15				The Wiske Water-troughs are taken at high speed. Speed is reduced approaching Darlington and we average 57.0 m.p.h. over this 14¼ miles. (See Map 18.)
DARLINGTON to FERRY HILL	12	1,496	16				The line rises 1 : 220 and 1 : 203 until we reach the summit by milepost 55, 292 feet above sea level. We average 47.4 m.p.h. over this section. (See Maps 18 and 19.)
FERRY HILL to DURHAM	9	330	12				Severe rising and falling gradients and speed restrictions limit our speed on this section, and we average 46.2 m.p.h. (See Maps 19 and 20.)
DURHAM to NEWCASTLE	14	66	19				This is not a fast section of the line and our average speed works out at 44.2 m.p.h. The approach to Newcastle over the King Edward Bridge is taken very slowly. (See Maps 20 and 21.)

(Continued on page 27)

13

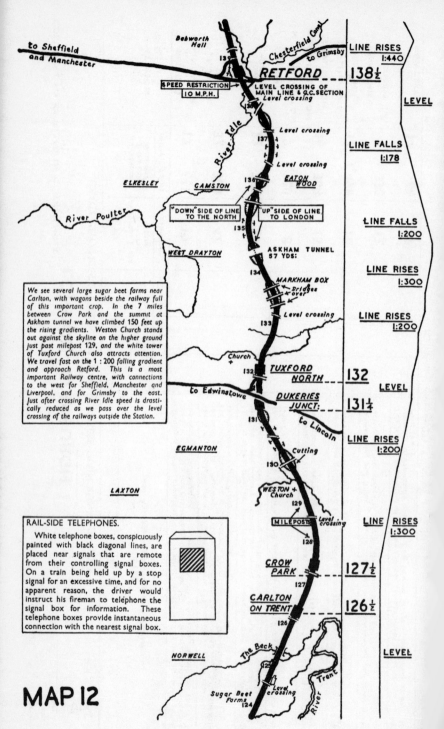

to Sheffield
and Manchester

Babworth Hall

131

Chesterfield Canal

to Grimsby

RETFORD

LINE RISES
1:440

138½

LEVEL

SPEED RESTRICTION
10 M.P.H.

LEVEL CROSSING OF
MAIN LINE & G.C. SECTION
Level crossing

Level crossing

LINE FALLS
1:178

137

River Idle

Level crossing

136

EATON
WOOD

ELKESLEY

GAMSTON

"DOWN" SIDE OF LINE
TO THE NORTH

"UP" SIDE OF LINE
TO LONDON

LINE FALLS
1:200

River Poulter

135

WEST DRAYTON

ASKHAM TUNNEL
57 YDS:

LINE RISES
1:300

134

MARKHAM BOX

Bridges over

LINE RISES
1:200

Level crossing

133

We see several large sugar beet farms near
Carlton, with wagons beside the railway full
of this important crop. In the 7 miles
between Crow Park and the summit at
Askham tunnel we have climbed 150 feet up
the rising gradients. Weston Church stands
out against the skyline on the higher ground
just past milepost 129, and the white tower
of Tuxford Church also attracts attention.
We travel fast on the 1 : 200 falling gradient
and approach Retford. This is a most
important Railway centre, with connections
to the west for Sheffield, Manchester and
Liverpool, and for Grimsby to the east.
Just after crossing River Idle speed is drastically reduced as we pass over the level
crossing of the railways outside the Station.

Church

132

**TUXFORD
NORTH**

132

LEVEL

to Edwinstowe

**DUKERIES
JUNCT:**

131¼

to Lincoln

131

LINE RISES
1:200

EGMANTON

130

Cutting

LAXTON

WESTON
Church

129

LINE RISES
1:300

MILEPOSTS

Level
crossing

128

RAIL-SIDE TELEPHONES.

White telephone boxes, conspicuously
painted with black diagonal lines, are
placed near signals that are remote
from their controlling signal boxes.
On a train being held up by a stop
signal for an excessive time, and for no
apparent reason, the driver would
instruct his fireman to telephone the
signal box for information. These
telephone boxes provide instantaneous
connection with the nearest signal box.

**CROW
PARK**

127½

127

**CARLTON
ON TRENT**

126½

126

NORWELL

The Beck

LEVEL

125

Trent

MAP 12

Sugar Beet
Farms

124

Level
crossing

River

14

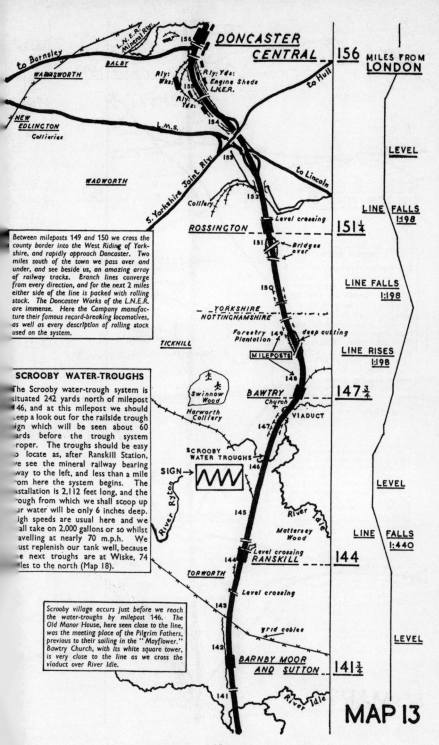

DONCASTER CENTRAL

156 MILES FROM **LONDON**

to Barnsley

L.N.E.R. Mineral Rly

WARMSWORTH

BALBY

156

Rly: Wks: Rly: Yds:

Rly: Yds: Engine Sheds
L.N.E.R.

155

to Hull

NEW
EDLINGTON
Collieries

Rly: Yds:

154

LEVEL

M.S.

153

to Lincoln

S. Yorkshire Joint Rly

WADWORTH

152

LINE FALLS
1:198

Colliery

Level crossing

151¼

ROSSINGTON

151

Bridges
over

LINE FALLS
1:198

150

YORKSHIRE
NOTTINGHAMSHIRE

deep cutting

LINE RISES
1:198

TICKHILL

Forestry 149
Plantation

MILEPOSTS

148

147¾

Swinnow
Wood

BAWTRY
Church

Harworth
Colliery

VIADUCT

147

SCROOBY
WATER TROUGHS

146

SIGN →

LEVEL

River Ryton

145

River Idle

Mattersey
Wood

LINE FALLS
1:440

144

Level crossing
RANSKILL

TORWORTH

143

Level crossing

grid cables

142

BARNBY MOOR
AND SUTTON

LEVEL

141¾

141

River Idle

MAP 13

Between mileposts 149 and 150 we cross the
county border into the West Riding of Yorkshire, and rapidly approach Doncaster. Two
miles south of the town we pass over and
under, and see beside us, an amazing array
of railway tracks. Branch lines converge
from every direction, and for the next 2 miles
either side of the line is packed with rolling
stock. The Doncaster Works of the L.N.E.R.
are immense. Here the Company manufac-
ture their famous record-breaking locomotives,
as well as every description of rolling stock
used on the system.

SCROOBY WATER-TROUGHS

The Scrooby water-trough system is
situated 242 yards north of milepost
146, and at this milepost we should
keep a look out for the railside trough
sign which will be seen about 60
yards before the trough system
proper. The troughs should be easy
to locate as, after Ranskill Station,
we see the mineral railway bearing
away to the left, and less than a mile
from here the system begins. The
installation is 2,112 feet long, and the
trough from which we shall scoop up
our water will be only 6 inches deep.
High speeds are usual here and we
shall take on 2,000 gallons or so whilst
travelling at nearly 70 m.p.h. We
must replenish our tank well, because
the next troughs are at Wiske, 74
miles to the north (Map 18).

Scrooby village occurs just before we reach
the water-troughs by milepost 146. The
Old Manor House, here seen close to the line,
was the meeting place of the Pilgrim Fathers,
previous to their sailing in the "Mayflower."
Bawtry Church, with its white square tower,
is very close to the line as we cross the
viaduct over River Idle.

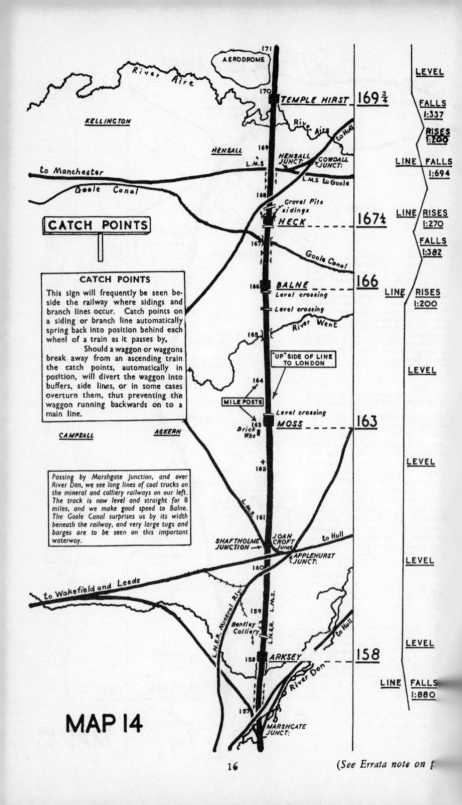

CATCH POINTS

CATCH POINTS

This sign will frequently be seen beside the railway where sidings and branch lines occur. Catch points on a siding or branch line automatically spring back into position behind each wheel of a train as it passes by,

Should a waggon or waggons break away from an ascending train the catch points, automatically in position, will divert the waggon into buffers, side lines, or in some cases overturn them, thus preventing the waggon running backwards on to a main line.

Passing by Marshgate Junction, and over River Don, we see long lines of coal trucks on the mineral and colliery railways on our left. The track is now level and straight for 8 miles, and we make good speed to Balne. The Goole Canal surprises us by its width beneath the railway, and very large tugs and barges are to be seen on this important waterway.

River Aire

AERODROME

171

170

TEMPLE HIRST 169¾

River Aire

to Hull

KELLINGTON

HENSALL 169

HENSALL JUNCT. **GOWDALL JUNCT.**

to Manchester L.M.S

LINE FALLS 1:694

L.M.S to Goole

Goole Canal

168

Gravel Pits sidings

HECK 167½

167

Goole Canal

166 **BALNE** 166

Level crossing

Level crossing

165

River Went

164

"UP" SIDE OF LINE TO LONDON

MILE POSTS

Level crossing

163 **MOSS** 163

Brick Wks

CAMPSALL **ASKERN**

+ 162

L.M.S 161

SHAFTHOLME JUNCTION → **JOAN CROFT JUNCT.** *to Hull*

APPLEHURST JUNCT.

160

to Wakefield and Leeds

L.N.E.R. Mineral Rly.

159

Bentley Colliery

L.N.E.R. L.M.S

to Hull

158 **ARKSEY** 158

River Don

157

MARSHGATE JUNCT.

MAP 14

LEVEL

FALLS 1:337

RISES 1:200

LINE RISES 1:270

FALLS 1:382

LINE RISES 1:200

LEVEL

LEVEL

LEVEL

LEVEL

LEVEL

LINE FALLS 1:880

16

(See Errata note on p

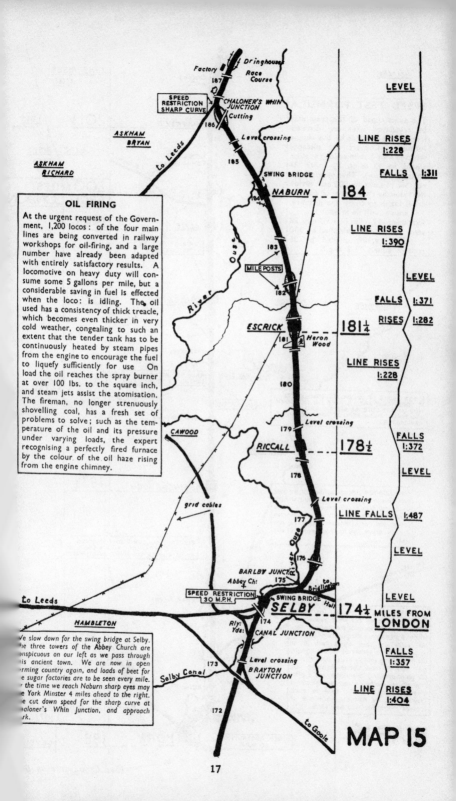

LEVEL

Factory
Dringhouses
Race Course

187

SPEED RESTRICTION SHARP CURVE

CHALONER'S WHIN JUNCTION

Cutting

186

LINE RISES 1:228

FALLS | 1:311

Level crossing

ASKHAM BRYAN

ASKHAM RICHARD

to Leeds

185

SWING BRIDGE

NABURN

184

184

LINE RISES 1:390

OIL FIRING

At the urgent request of the Government, 1,200 locos: of the four main lines are being converted in railway workshops for oil-firing, and a large number have already been adapted with entirely satisfactory results. A locomotive on heavy duty will consume some 5 gallons per mile, but a considerable saving in fuel is effected when the loco: is idling. The oil used has a consistency of thick treacle, which becomes even thicker in very cold weather, congealing to such an extent that the tender tank has to be continuously heated by steam pipes from the engine to encourage the fuel to liquefy sufficiently for use. On load the oil reaches the spray burner at over 100 lbs. to the square inch, and steam jets assist the atomisation. The fireman, no longer strenuously shovelling coal, has a fresh set of problems to solve; such as the temperature of the oil and its pressure under varying loads, the expert recognising a perfectly fired furnace by the colour of the oil haze rising from the engine chimney.

183

MILE POSTS

182

LEVEL

FALLS | 1:371

RISES | 1:282

ESCRICK

181

181¼

181¼

Heron Wood

LINE RISES 1:228

180

River Ouse

Level crossing

179

RICCALL

178½

178½

FALLS | 1:372

LEVEL

178

CAWOOD

grid cables

Level crossing

177

LINE FALLS | 1:487

River Ouse

176

LEVEL

BARLBY JUNCN

Abbey Ch:
175

to Bridlington
Hull

LEVEL

SPEED RESTRICTION 30 M.P.H.

SWING BRIDGE

SELBY

174

174½

174½

MILES FROM **LONDON**

to Leeds

HAMBLETON

Rly: Yds:

CANAL JUNCTION

FALLS | 1:357

We slow down for the swing bridge at Selby. The three towers of the **Abbey** Church are conspicuous on our left as we pass through this ancient town. We are now in open farming country again, and loads of beet for the sugar factories are to be seen every mile. By the time we reach Naburn sharp eyes may see York Minster 4 miles ahead to the right. We cut down speed for the sharp curve at Chaloner's Whin Junction, and approach York.

173

Level crossing

BRAYTON JUNCTION

Selby Canal

172

LINE RISES | 1:404

to Goole

MAP 15

17

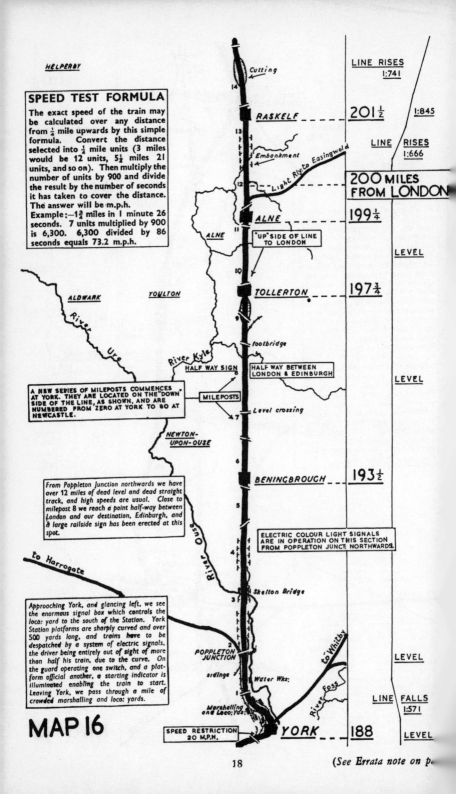

(See Errata note on p.

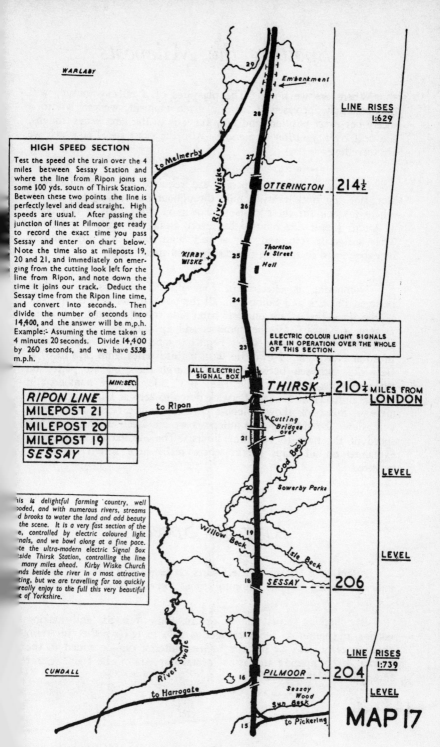

WARLABY

HIGH SPEED SECTION

Test the speed of the train over the 4 miles between Sessay Station and where the line from Ripon joins us some 100 yds. south of Thirsk Station. Between these two points the line is perfectly level and dead straight. High speeds are usual. After passing the junction of lines at Pilmoor get ready to record the exact time you pass Sessay and enter on chart below. Note the time also at mileposts 19, 20 and 21, and immediately on emerging from the cutting look left for the line from Ripon, and note down the time it joins our track. Deduct the Sessay time from the Ripon line time, and convert into seconds. Then divide the number of seconds into 14,400, and the answer will be m.p.h. Example:- Assuming the time taken is 4 minutes 20 seconds. Divide 14,400 by 260 seconds, and we have 55.38 m.p.h.

	MIN: SEC.
RIPON LINE	
MILEPOST 21	
MILEPOST 20	
MILEPOST 19	
SESSAY	

to Ripon

his is delightful farming country, well ...ooded, and with numerous rivers, streams ...d brooks to water the land and add beauty ... the scene. It is a very fast section of the ...e, controlled by electric coloured light ...nals, and we bowl along at a fine pace. ...te the ultra-modern electric Signal Box ...side Thirsk Station, controlling the line ... many miles ahead. Kirby Wiske Church ...nds beside the river in a most attractive ...ing, but we are travelling far too quickly ...really enjoy to the full this very beautiful ...t of Yorkshire.

CUNDALL

River Swale

to Harrogate

to Melmerby

River Wiske

KIRBY WISKE

Embankment

OTTERINGTON

Thornton le Street Hall

ELECTRIC COLOUR LIGHT SIGNALS ARE IN OPERATION OVER THE WHOLE OF THIS SECTION.

ALL ELECTRIC SIGNAL BOX

THIRSK

Cutting Bridges over

Cod Beck

Sowerby Parks

Willow Beck

Isle Beck

SESSAY

PILMOOR

Sessay Wood

Sun Beck

to Pickering

LINE RISES 1:629

214½

210¼ MILES FROM LONDON

LEVEL

LEVEL

206

LINE RISES 1:739

204

LEVEL

MAP 17

Spotting the Mileposts

Where are we now? The pleasures of a railway journey will be immensely increased if, at any given moment, we can tell to a nicety our exact position, and how far it is to the next water-troughs, the next river, junction or Station. Also the exact speed at which we are travelling.

By law, Railway Companies are required to place mile posts alongside the track every $\frac{1}{4}$ mile throughout the system, and exactly where to look for these posts is shown on every map in this book. $\frac{1}{4}$, $\frac{1}{2}$ and $\frac{3}{4}$ posts are omitted but every actual mile post is indicated. They are easily seen, and only at very high speeds will any difficulty be experienced in spotting the clearly numbered posts.

Numbering is effected in four distinct sections and, except between Berwick and Edinburgh, all the posts are on the "down" side of the line—that is, on our left hand side travelling north. Starting at zero at Kings Cross the numbers add up until we reach post 188 at York. Here another series begins numbered from zero at York to 80 at Newcastle. Newcastle starts a third series from zero to 67 at Berwick. Between Berwick and Edinburgh the posts are placed on the opposite side of the line, the "up" side, and are numbered in reverse order from 57 near Berwick down to zero at Edinburgh. The maps in this book show milepost positions as accurately as the scale will allow. By spotting the mileposts we can ascertain and check the speed of the train to very fine limits. The method of so doing is explained on all maps herein where really high speeds are to be expected.

Average Speeds

Attention is drawn to the Charts on pages 5, 13 and 27, which indicate normal express running times between principal Stations.

By checking actual times against those printed, and making entries in column 4, the passenger is able to tell whether his train running early, late, or to time. Great interest can be added to the journey by comparing the actual average speeds of the train against those given in the Charts.

On Other Pages

Signals ... ... Page 22.

Track Circuits ... ... Map 10.

Water Troughs ... ... Maps 5, 9, 11, 13, 18 and 23.

Catch Points ... ... Map 14.

High Speed Sections ... Maps 6, 8, 11, 17 and 23.

Tunnels ... ... Maps 4, 5, 10, 12, 26 and 28.

Mail-bag Pickups ... ... Maps, 7, 22 and 26.

Rail-side Telephones ... Map 12.

Speed Test Formula ... Maps 9, 16, 19, and 24.

Express Running Times ... Pages 5, 13 and 27.

Oil-burning Locos ... ... Map 15.

Coal Dues ... ... Map 4.

Speed Averages ... ... Pages 5, 13 and 27.

SEMAPHORE SIGNALS

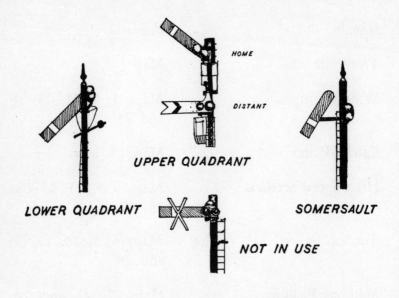

HOME

DISTANT

UPPER QUADRANT

LOWER QUADRANT

SOMERSAULT

NOT IN USE

COLOUR LIGHT SIGNALS

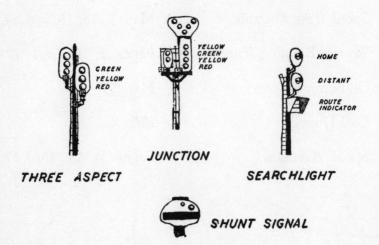

GREEN
YELLOW
RED

YELLOW
GREEN
YELLOW
RED

HOME

DISTANT

ROUTE
INDICATOR

JUNCTION

THREE ASPECT

SEARCHLIGHT

SHUNT SIGNAL

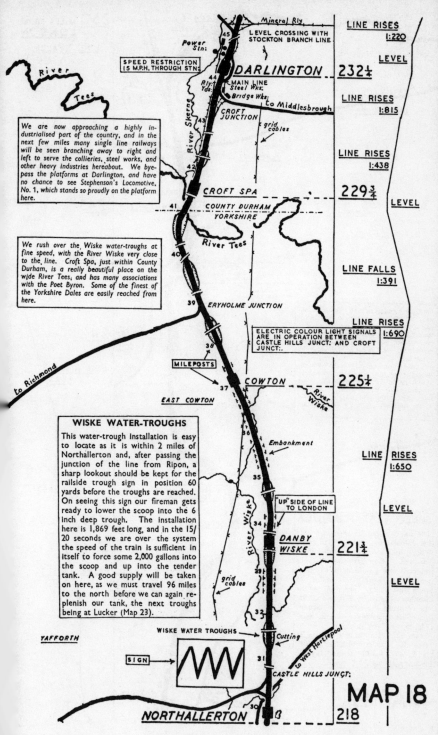

LINE RISES 1:220

LEVEL 232½

Mineral Rly.

LEVEL CROSSING WITH STOCKTON BRANCH LINE

Power Stn: 45

DARLINGTON

SPEED RESTRICTION 15 M.P.H. THROUGH STN:

44 MAIN LINE Steel Wks:
Rly. Bridge Wks:
Yds: To Middlesbrough

LINE RISES 1:815

CROFT JUNCTION

43 grid cables

LINE RISES 1:438

River Skerne

We are now approaching a highly industrialised part of the country, and in the next few miles many single line railways will be seen branching away to right and left to serve the collieries, steel works, and other heavy industries hereabout. We bypass the platforms at Darlington, and have no chance to see Stephenson's Locomotive, No. 1, which stands so proudly on the platform here.

42

CROFT SPA 229¾

LEVEL

41 COUNTY DURHAM
YORKSHIRE

River Tees

40

We rush over the Wiske water-troughs at fine speed, with the River Wiske very close to the line. Croft Spa, just within County Durham, is a really beautiful place on the wide River Tees, and has many associations with the Poet Byron. Some of the finest of the Yorkshire Dales are easily reached from here.

LINE FALLS 1:391

39 ERYHOLME JUNCTION

LINE RISES 1:690

ELECTRIC COLOUR LIGHT SIGNALS ARE IN OPERATION BETWEEN CASTLE HILLS JUNCT: AND CROFT JUNCT:.

to Richmond

38

MILEPOSTS

37 COWTON 225½

EAST COWTON

River Wiske

WISKE WATER-TROUGHS

This water-trough installation is easy to locate as it is within 2 miles of Northallerton and, after passing the junction of the line from Ripon, a sharp lookout should be kept for the railside trough sign in position 60 yards before the troughs are reached. On seeing this sign our fireman gets ready to lower the scoop into the 6 inch deep trough. The installation here is 1,869 feet long, and in the 15/20 seconds we are over the system the speed of the train is sufficient in itself to force some 2,000 gallons into the scoop and up into the tender tank. A good supply will be taken on here, as we must travel 96 miles to the north before we can again replenish our tank, the next troughs being at Lucker (Map 23).

Embankment

LINE RISES 1:650

35

LEVEL

"UP" SIDE OF LINE TO LONDON

34 DANBY WISKE 221¾

LEVEL

River Wiske

grid cables

33

32

YAFFORTH

WISKE WATER TROUGHS Cutting

to West Hartlepool

SIGN

31 CASTLE HILLS JUNCT:

MAP 18

30 218

NORTHALLERTON

23

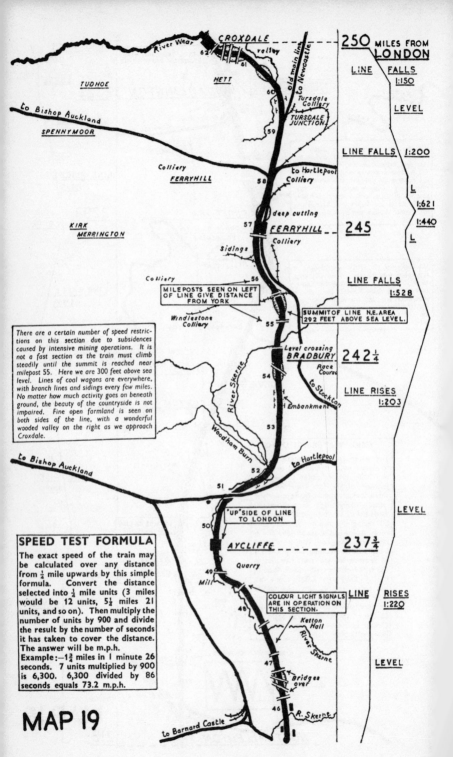

CROXDALE

River Wear

TUDHOE

to Bishop Auckland
SPENNYMOOR

Colliery
FERRYHILL

KIRK
MERRINGTON

Colliery

Sidings

MILEPOSTS SEEN ON LEFT
OF LINE GIVE DISTANCE
FROM YORK

*Windlestone
Colliery*

There are a certain number of speed restrictions on this section due to subsidences caused by intensive mining operations. It is not a fast section as the train must climb steadily until the summit is reached near milepost 55. Here we are 300 feet above sea level. Lines of coal wagons are everywhere, with branch lines and sidings every few miles. No matter how much activity goes on beneath ground, the beauty of the countryside is not impaired. Fine open farmland is seen on both sides of the line, with a wonderful wooded valley on the right as we approach Croxdale.

to Bishop Auckland

HETT

valley

old main line
to Newcastle

Tursdale
Colliery
TURSDALE
JUNCTION

to Hartlepool
Colliery

deep cutting
FERRYHILL
Colliery

River Skerne

SUMMIT OF LINE N.E. AREA
292 FEET ABOVE SEA LEVEL.

Level crossing
BRADBURY
Race
Course

to Stockton

Embankment

Woodham Burn

to Hartlepool

'UP' SIDE OF LINE
TO LONDON

AYCLIFFE

Quarry

Mill

COLOUR LIGHT SIGNALS
ARE IN OPERATION ON
THIS SECTION

Ketton
Hall

River Skerne

Bridges
over

R. Skerne

to Barnard Castle

250 MILES FROM
LONDON

LINE   FALLS
1:150

LEVEL

LINE FALLS   1:200

L
1:621

245
1:440

L

LINE FALLS
1:528

242¼

LINE RISES
1:203

LEVEL

237¾

LINE   RISES
1:220

LEVEL

SPEED TEST FORMULA

The exact speed of the train may be calculated over any distance from ¼ mile upwards by this simple formula.   Convert the distance selected into ¼ mile units (3 miles would be 12 units, 5¼ miles 21 units, and so on).   Then multiply the number of units by 900 and divide the result by the number of seconds it has taken to cover the distance. The answer will be m.p.h.
Example :—1¾ miles in 1 minute 26 seconds.   7 units multiplied by 900 is 6,300.   6,300 divided by 86 seconds equals 73.2 m.p.h.

MAP 19

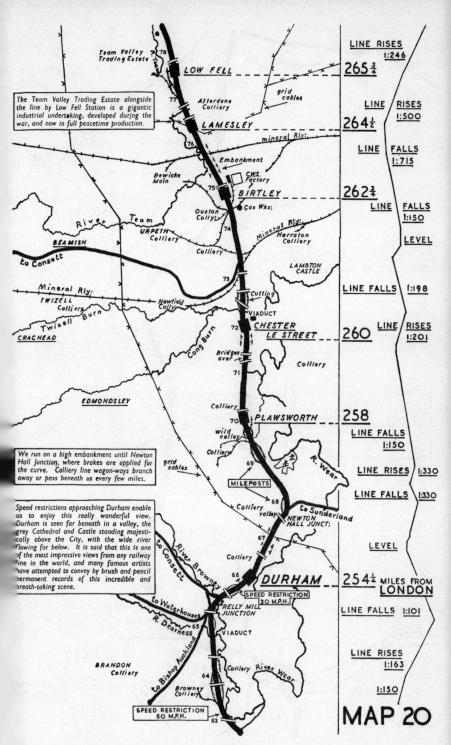

LINE RISES 1:246

265¾

Team Valley Trading Estate

78

LOW FELL

grid cables

The Team Valley Trading Estate alongside the line by Low Fell Station is a gigantic industrial undertaking, developed during the war, and now in full peacetime production.

77

Allerdene Colliery

LINE RISES 1:500

LAMESLEY

264½

76

mineral Rly:

Embankment

LINE FALLS 1:715

Bewicke Main

C.W.S. Factory

75

BIRTLEY

262¼

Ouston Colly:

Gas Wks:

LINE FALLS 1:150

River Team

URPETH Colliery

74

Mineral Rly:

Harraton Colliery

LEVEL

BEAMISH

To Consett

Colliery

LAMBTON CASTLE

73

LINE FALLS 1:198

Mineral Rly:

TWIZELL Colliery

Nawfield Colly:

Cutting

VIADUCT

260

LINE RISES 1:201

Twizell Burn

72

CHESTER LE STREET

CRAGHEAD

Cong Burn

Bridges over

71

Colliery

EDMONDSLEY

Colliery

70

PLAWSWORTH

258

wild valley

LINE FALLS 1:150

Colliery

We run on a high embankment until Newton Hall Junction, where brakes are applied for the curve. Colliery line wagon-ways branch away or pass beneath us every few miles.

grid cables

69

R. Wear

LINE RISES 1:330

MILEPOSTS

68

Colliery valley

to Sunderland

LINE FALLS 1:330

NEWTON HALL JUNCT:

Speed restrictions approaching Durham enable us to enjoy this really wonderful view. Durham is seen far beneath in a valley, the grey Cathedral and Castle standing majestically above the City, with the wide river flowing far below. It is said that this is one of the most impressive views from any railway line in the world, and many famous artists have attempted to convey by brush and pencil permanent records of this incredible and breath-taking scene.

67

LEVEL

River Browney

to Consett

Colliery

66

DURHAM

254¼ MILES FROM **LONDON**

SPEED RESTRICTION 30 M.P.H.

RELLY MILL JUNCTION

to Waterhouses

LINE FALLS 1:101

R. Deorness

65

VIADUCT

BRANDON Colliery

to Bishop Auckland

Colliery River Wear

LINE RISES 1:163

64

Browney Colliery

1:150

SPEED RESTRICTION 50 M.P.H.

63

MAP 20

25

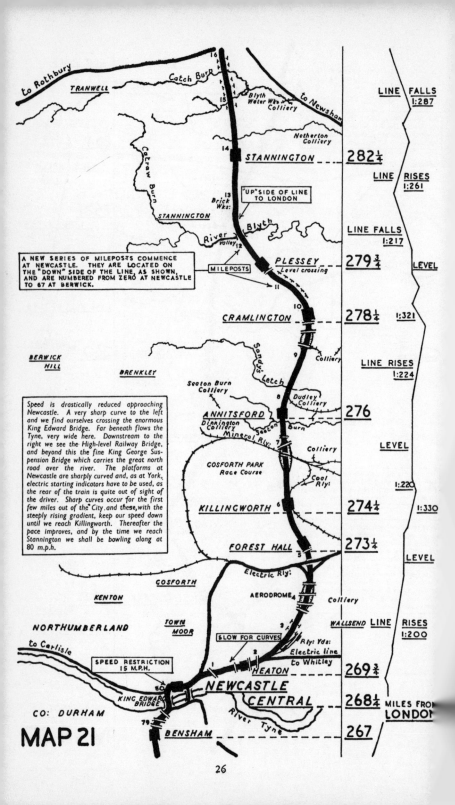

to Rothbury

TRANWELL

Catch Burn

to Newsham

Blyth Water Wks
Colliery

Netherton
Colliery

LINE FALLS
1:287

STANNINGTON

282¼

LINE RISES
1:261

Brick
Wks:

"UP" SIDE OF LINE
TO LONDON

STANNINGTON

River Blyth

Valley

LINE FALLS
1:217

Catraw Burn

MILEPOSTS

PLESSEY
Level crossing

279¾

LEVEL

A NEW SERIES OF MILEPOSTS COMMENCE AT NEWCASTLE. THEY ARE LOCATED ON THE "DOWN" SIDE OF THE LINE, AS SHOWN, AND ARE NUMBERED FROM ZERO AT NEWCASTLE TO 67 AT BERWICK.

CRAMLINGTON

278¼

1:321

BERWICK
HILL

BRENKLEY

Sandys Letch

Colliery

LINE RISES
1:224

Seaton Burn
Colliery

Dudley
Colliery

ANNITSFORD

276

Speed is drastically reduced approaching Newcastle. A very sharp curve to the left and we find ourselves crossing the enormous King Edward Bridge. Far beneath flows the Tyne, very wide here. Downstream to the right we see the High-level Railway Bridge, and beyond this the fine King George Suspension Bridge which carries the great north road over the river. The platforms at Newcastle are sharply curved and, as at York, electric starting indicators have to be used, as the rear of the train is quite out of sight of the driver. Sharp curves occur for the first few miles out of the City and these, with the steeply rising gradient, keep our speed down until we reach Killingworth. Thereafter the pace improves, and by the time we reach Stannington we shall be bowling along at 80 m.p.h.

Dinnington Colliery

Seaton Burn
Mineral Rly:

Colliery

LEVEL

GOSFORTH PARK
Race Course

Coal Rly:

1:220

KILLINGWORTH

274¼

1:330

FOREST HALL

273¼

LEVEL

Electric Rly:

GOSFORTH

KENTON

AERODROME

Colliery

NORTHUMBERLAND

TOWN
MOOR

WALLSEND LINE RISES
1:200

to Carlisle

SLOW FOR CURVES

Rly: Yds:
Electric line
to Whitley

SPEED RESTRICTION
15 M.P.H.

HEATON

269¾

NEWCASTLE CENTRAL

268¼

MILES FROM
LONDON

CO: DURHAM

KING EDWARD
BRIDGE

River Tyne

267

MAP 21

BENSHAM

LONDON—EDINBURGH

EXACT DISTANCES BETWEEN STATIONS—EXPRESS TRAIN RUNNING TIMES

(1) STATION	(2) Distance Between Stations		(3) Express Train Running Times	(4) Actual Running Times			(5) NOTES and Average Speeds over each Section
	Miles	Yards	Minutes	Minutes	Early	Late	
NEWCASTLE to MORPETH	16	1,100	28				From a standing start we commence slowly, and for several miles our speed is restricted by curves. Rising gradients for 10 miles keep down our progress. High speeds are attained after Cramlington, but we must slow down for the curve at Morpeth. Average 35.5 m.p.h. (See Maps 21 and 22.)
MORPETH to ALNMOUTH	18	418	20				This is quite a fast section, particularly between Widdrington and Acklington, and on testing we shall find we are travelling at nearer 80 than 70 m.p.h. We average 54.7 m.p.h. over this 18¼ miles. (See Maps 22 and 23.)
ALNMOUTH to BELFORD	16	1,385	18				After climbing for 4 miles we make fine speed down the 1:150 gradient and passing over the Lucker Water-troughs at nearly 70 m.p.h., maintaining this speed to Belford. Average speed 55.8 m.p.h. (See Maps 23 and 24.)
BELFORD to BERWICK	15	616	18				The line falls all the way to Goswick and we make fine speed. The approach to Berwick through Tweedmouth and over the Royal Border Bridge is taken very slowly. (Average speed 51.6 m.p.h. (See Maps 24 and 25.)
BERWICK to RESTON	11	484	17				From a standing start we travel slowly up the 1:190 gradient past the border of England and Scotland. Once over the summit, near Ayton, we make fine progress. Average speed only 39.7 m.p.h. (See Map 25.)
RESTON to DUNBAR	17	—	21				Speed is not high for the first 5 miles of this section due to the rising gradients, but it is very high from Penmanshiel tunnel onwards. We approach Dunbar slowly. Average speed 48.5 m.p.h. (See Maps 25 and 26.)
DUNBAR to DREM	11	880	13				Although the gradients are not favourable, this is, nevertheless, a fast 11½ miles, and we average 53 m.p.h. (See Maps 26 and 27.)
DREM to WAVERLEY	17	1,320	30				Speed is high as far as Inveresk, but from here we slow down considerably as we approach Edinburgh. We climb a severe 1:98 gradient over the last 1¼ miles. Average speed works out at 35.5 m.p.h. (See Maps 27 and 28.)

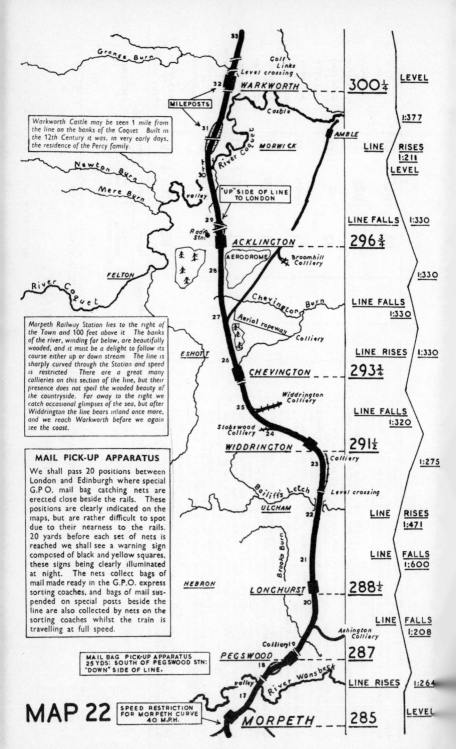

Grange Burn

33

Golf Links

Level crossing

WARKWORTH

32

MILEPOSTS

Warkworth Castle may be seen 1 mile from
the line on the banks of the Coquet. Built in
the 12th Century it was, in very early days,
the residence of the Percy family.

31

Castle

AMBLE

MORWICK

Newton Burn

Mere Burn

30

River Coquet

valley

"UP" SIDE OF LINE
TO LONDON

29

Radio
Stn.

ACKLINGTON

FELTON

AERODROME

Broomhill
Colliery

28

River Coquet

Chevington Burn

27

Aerial ropeway

Colliery

ESHOTT

26

Morpeth Railway Station lies to the right of
the Town and 100 feet above it. The banks
of the river, winding far below, are beautifully
wooded, and it must be a delight to follow its
course either up or down stream. The line is
sharply curved through the Station and speed
is restricted. There are a great many
collieries on this section of the line, but their
presence does not spoil the wooded beauty of
the countryside. Far away to the right we
catch occasional glimpses of the sea, but after
Widdrington the line bears inland once more,
and we reach Warkworth before we again
see the coast.

CHEVINGTON

Widdrington
Colliery

25

Stobswood
Colliery 24

WIDDRINGTON

23

Colliery

MAIL PICK-UP APPARATUS

We shall pass 20 positions between
London and Edinburgh where special
G.P.O. mail bag catching nets are
erected close beside the rails. These
positions are clearly indicated on the
maps, but are rather difficult to spot
due to their nearness to the rails.
20 yards before each set of nets is
reached we shall see a warning sign
composed of black and yellow squares,
these signs being clearly illuminated
at night. The nets collect bags of
mail made ready in the G.P.O. express
sorting coaches, and bags of mail suspended on special posts beside the
line are also collected by nets on the
sorting coaches whilst the train is
travelling at full speed.

Bailiff's Letch

Level crossing

ULGHAM

22

Brooks Burn

HEBRON

21

LONGHURST

20

Ashington
Colliery

MAIL BAG PICK-UP APPARATUS
25 YDS. SOUTH OF PEGSWOOD STN.
"DOWN" SIDE OF LINE.

Colliery 19

PEGSWOOD

18

River Wansbeck

MAP 22

SPEED RESTRICTION
FOR MORPETH CURVE
40 M.P.H.

valley 17

MORPETH

LEVEL   300¼

1:377

LINE   RISES
1:211

LEVEL

LINE FALLS 1:330

296¾

1:330

LINE FALLS
1:330

LINE RISES 1:330

293¼

LINE FALLS
1:320

291½

1:275

LINE   RISES
1:471

LINE   FALLS
1:600   288½

LINE   FALLS
1:208

287

LINE RISES   1:264

LEVEL   285

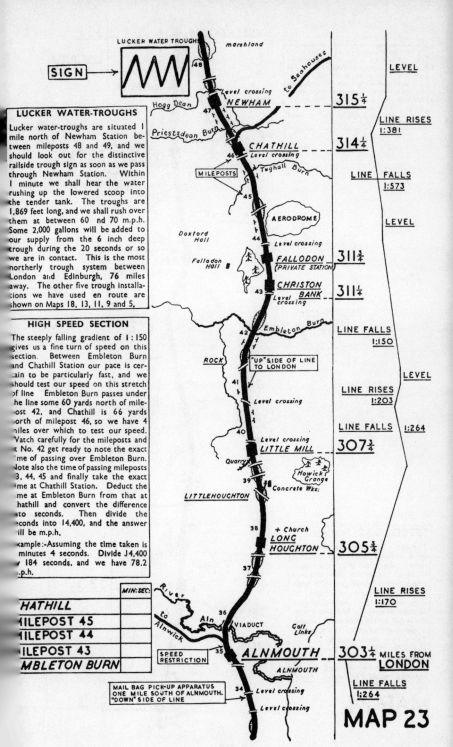

SIGN → LUCKER WATER TROUGHS

LUCKER WATER-TROUGHS

Lucker water-troughs are situated 1 mile north of Newham Station between mileposts 48 and 49, and we should look out for the distinctive railside trough sign as soon as we pass through Newham Station. Within 1 minute we shall hear the water rushing up the lowered scoop into the tender tank. The troughs are 1,869 feet long, and we shall rush over them at between 60 and 70 m.p.h. Some 2,000 gallons will be added to our supply from the 6 inch deep trough during the 20 seconds or so we are in contact. This is the most northerly trough system between London and Edinburgh, 76 miles away. The other five trough installations we have used en route are shown on Maps 18, 13, 11, 9 and 5.

HIGH SPEED SECTION

The steeply falling gradient of 1 : 150 gives us a fine turn of speed on this section. Between Embleton Burn and Chathill Station our pace is certain to be particularly fast, and we should test our speed on this stretch of line. Embleton Burn passes under the line some 60 yards north of milepost 42, and Chathill is 66 yards north of milepost 46, so we have 4 miles over which to test our speed. Watch carefully for the mileposts and at No. 42 get ready to note the exact time of passing over Embleton Burn. Note also the time of passing mileposts 43, 44, 45 and finally take the exact time at Chathill Station. Deduct the time at Embleton Burn from that at Chathill and convert the difference into seconds. Then divide the seconds into 14,400, and the answer will be m.p.h.

Example:—Assuming the time taken is 3 minutes 4 seconds. Divide 14,400 by 184 seconds, and we have 78.2 m.p.h.

	MIN: SEC:
CHATHILL	
MILEPOST 45	
MILEPOST 44	
MILEPOST 43	
EMBLETON BURN	

SPEED RESTRICTION

MAIL BAG PICK-UP APPARATUS ONE MILE SOUTH OF ALNMOUTH. "DOWN" SIDE OF LINE.

marshland

to Seahouses

Hogg Dean

Level crossing

NEWHAM

Priestsdean Burn

CHATHILL

Level crossing

MILEPOSTS

Tughall Burn

AERODROME

Doxford Hall

Level crossing

Fallodon Hall

FALLODON
(PRIVATE STATION)

CHRISTON BANK

Level crossing

Embleton Burn

ROCK

"UP" SIDE OF LINE TO LONDON

Level crossing

Level crossing

LITTLE MILL

Quarry

Howick Grange

LITTLEHOUGHTON

Concrete Wks.

+ Church

LONG HOUGHTON

River

to Alnwick

Aln

VIADUCT

Golf Links

ALNMOUTH

ALNMOUTH

Level crossing

Level crossing

LEVEL

315¼

LINE RISES 1:381

314¼

LINE FALLS 1:573

LEVEL

311¾

311¼

LINE FALLS 1:150

LEVEL

LINE RISES 1:203

LINE FALLS 1:264

307¾

305¾

LINE RISES 1:170

303¼ MILES FROM LONDON

LINE FALLS 1:264

MAP 23

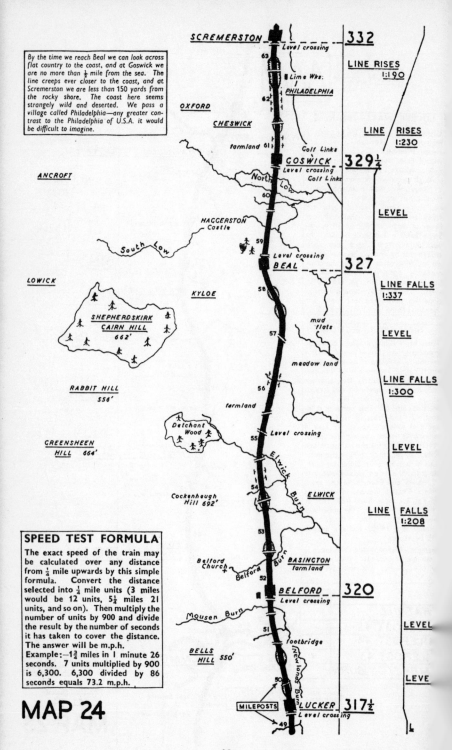

By the time we reach Beal we can look across flat country to the coast, and at Goswick we are no more than ½ mile from the sea. The line creeps ever closer to the coast, and at Scremerston we are less than 150 yards from the rocky shore. The coast here seems strangely wild and deserted. We pass a village called Philadelphia—any greater contrast to the Philadelphia of U.S.A. it would be difficult to imagine.

SCREMERSTON   332

Level crossing

63

Lime Wks.

PHILADELPHIA

LINE RISES
1:190

62

OXFORD

CHESWICK

farmland 61

Golf Links

COSWICK   329½

Level crossing

Golf Links

ANCROFT

North Low

LINE RISES
1:230

60

LEVEL

HAGGERSTON
Castle

59

South Low

Level crossing

BEAL   327

LOWICK

KYLOE

58

LINE FALLS
1:337

SHEPHERDSKIRK
CAIRN HILL
662'

mud flats

57

LEVEL

meadow land

RABBIT HILL
556'

56

LINE FALLS
1:300

farmland

GREENSHEEN
HILL 664'

Detchant
Wood

55

Level crossing

LEVEL

Elwick Burn

54

ELWICK

Cockenheugh
Hill 692'

53

LINE FALLS
1:208

SPEED TEST FORMULA

The exact speed of the train may be calculated over any distance from ¼ mile upwards by this simple formula. Convert the distance selected into ¼ mile units (3 miles would be 12 units, 5¼ miles 21 units, and so on). Then multiply the number of units by 900 and divide the result by the number of seconds it has taken to cover the distance. The answer will be m.p.h.

Example:—1¾ miles in 1 minute 26 seconds. 7 units multiplied by 900 is 6,300. 6,300 divided by 86 seconds equals 73.2 m.p.h.

Belford Church

Belford Burn

BASINGTON
farmland

52

BELFORD   320

Level crossing

Mousen Burn

51

footbridge

LEVEL

BELLS
HILL 550'

New Jonns Burn

50

LEVE

MAP 24

MILEPOSTS

LUCKER   317½

Level crossing

49

30

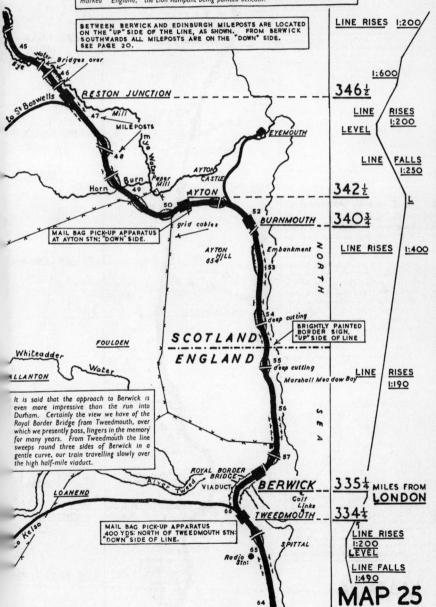

THE BORDER

Three miles north of Berwick, between mileposts 54 and 55, a brightly painted sign indicates the exact position of the boundary between England and Scotland. The sign is placed against a low stone wall on the "up" side of the line, and is easily visible from the train. Deep cuttings occur both to the north and south of the boundary, momentarily spoiling our view of the sea. On emerging into the clear from either cutting we should keep a sharp look out. On one side of the sign is painted the Scottish Unicorn, with above an arm marked "Scotland," pointing northwards. The other side shows a similar arm pointing southwards marked "England," the Lion Rampant being painted beneath.

BETWEEN BERWICK AND EDINBURGH MILEPOSTS ARE LOCATED ON THE "UP" SIDE OF THE LINE, AS SHOWN. FROM BERWICK SOUTHWARDS ALL MILEPOSTS ARE ON THE "DOWN" SIDE. SEE PAGE 20.

LINE RISES 1:200

1:600

RESTON JUNCTION

346½

LINE RISES 1:200

LINE LEVEL

EYEMOUTH

LINE FALLS 1:250

to St Boswells

45

Eye Water

Bridges over

46

47 Mill

MILEPOSTS

Eye Water

48

Burn

Horn 49

Paper Mill

AYTON CASTLE

342½

50

AYTON

52

BURNMOUTH

340¾

grid cables

MAIL BAG PICK-UP APPARATUS AT AYTON STN. "DOWN" SIDE.

AYTON HILL 654

Embankment

53

LINE RISES 1:400

NORTH

54 deep cutting

BRIGHTLY PAINTED BORDER SIGN, "UP" SIDE OF LINE

FOULDEN

SCOTLAND

ENGLAND

Whiteadder

55 deep cutting

Water

ALLANTON

Marshall Meadow Bay

LINE RISES 1:190

It is said that the approach to Berwick is even more impressive than the run into Durham. Certainly the view we have of the Royal Border Bridge from Tweedmouth, over which we presently pass, lingers in the memory for many years. From Tweedmouth the line sweeps round three sides of Berwick in a gentle curve, our train travelling slowly over the high half-mile viaduct.

56

SEA

57

ROYAL BORDER BRIDGE

River Tweed

VIADUCT

LOANEND

BERWICK

335¼ MILES FROM LONDON

Golf Links

to Kelso

66

TWEEDMOUTH

334¼

MAIL BAG PICK-UP APPARATUS 400 YDS: NORTH OF TWEEDMOUTH STN: "DOWN" SIDE OF LINE.

SPITTAL

LINE RISES 1:200

LEVEL

65

Radio Stn:

LINE FALLS 1:490

64

MAP 25

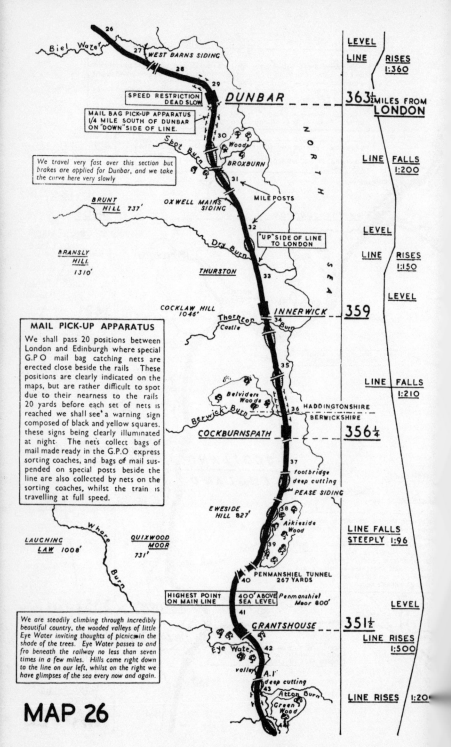

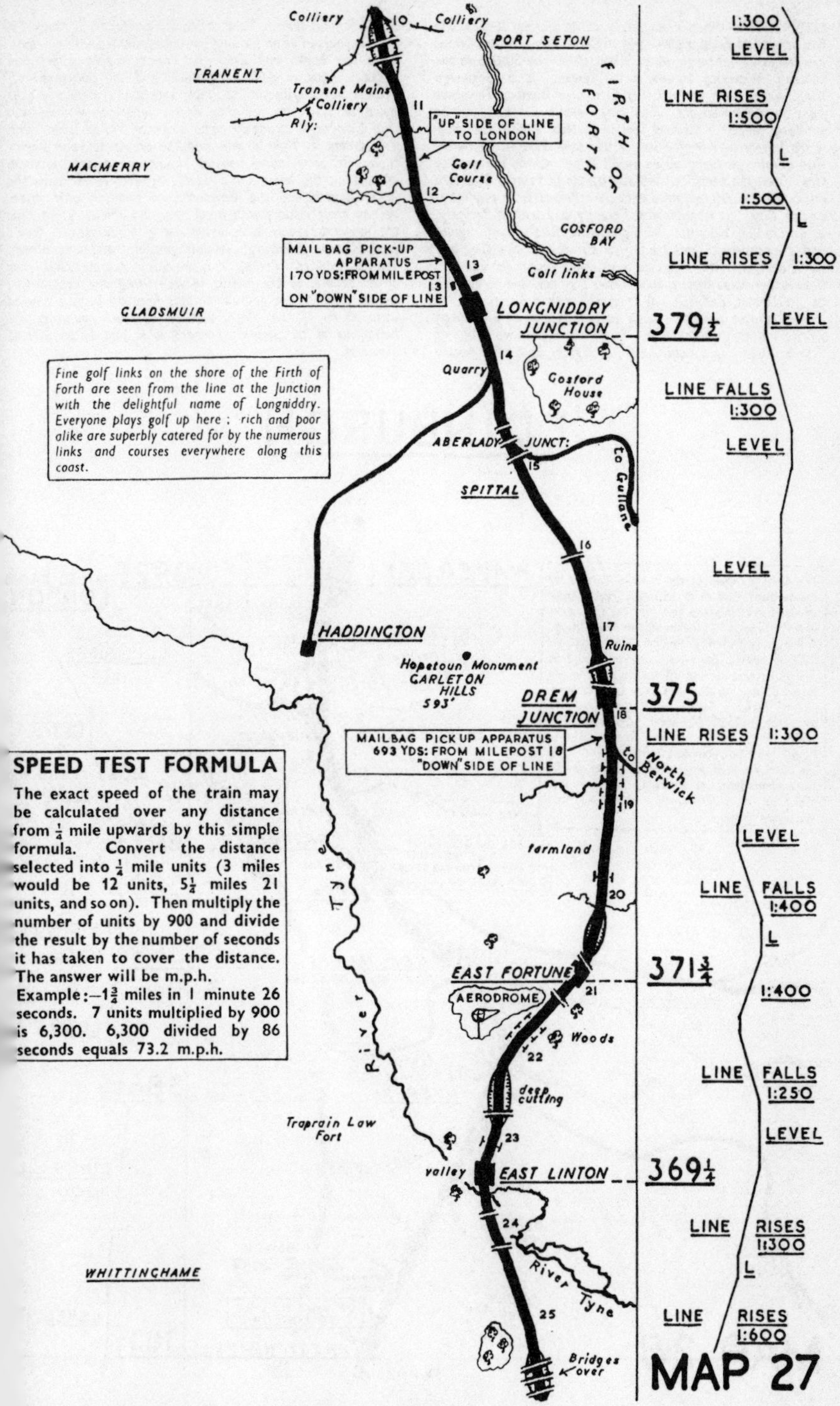

Colliery
10
Colliery
PORT SETON
FIRTH OF FORTH
TRANENT
Tranent Mains Colliery Rly:
11
"UP" SIDE OF LINE TO LONDON
MACMERRY
Golf Course
12
GOSFORD BAY
MAILBAG PICK-UP APPARATUS 170 YDS: FROM MILEPOST 13 ON "DOWN" SIDE OF LINE
13
Golf links
GLADSMUIR
LONGNIDDRY JUNCTION
14
Quarry
Gosford House
ABERLADY JUNCT:
to Gullane
15
SPITTAL
16
17
Ruins
HADDINGTON
Hopetoun Monument
GARLETON HILLS 593'
DREM JUNCTION
18
MAILBAG PICK UP APPARATUS 693 YDS: FROM MILEPOST 18 "DOWN" SIDE OF LINE
to North Berwick
19
farmland
River Tyne
20
EAST FORTUNE
AERODROME
21
Woods
22
deep cutting
Traprain Law Fort
23
valley
EAST LINTON
24
River Tyne
WHITTINGHAME
25
Bridges over
1:300
LEVEL
LINE RISES 1:500
L
1:500
L
LINE RISES 1:300
379½
LEVEL
LINE FALLS 1:300
LEVEL
LEVEL
375
LINE RISES 1:300
LEVEL
LINE FALLS 1:400
L
371¾
1:400
LINE FALLS 1:250
LEVEL
369¼
LINE RISES 1:300
L
LINE RISES 1:600
MAP 27

Fine golf links on the shore of the Firth of Forth are seen from the line at the Junction with the delightful name of Longniddry. Everyone plays golf up here; rich and poor alike are superbly catered for by the numerous links and courses everywhere along this coast.

SPEED TEST FORMULA

The exact speed of the train may be calculated over any distance from ¼ mile upwards by this simple formula. Convert the distance selected into ¼ mile units (3 miles would be 12 units, 5¼ miles 21 units, and so on). Then multiply the number of units by 900 and divide the result by the number of seconds it has taken to cover the distance. The answer will be m.p.h.
Example:—1¾ miles in 1 minute 26 seconds. 7 units multiplied by 900 is 6,300. 6,300 divided by 86 seconds equals 73.2 m.p.h.

EDINBURGH—When one arrives at Waverley Station one has arrived in Edinburgh—right in Edinburgh. No taxi rides are necessary through dingy streets from the Station to the centre ; Waverley Station is the centre. It is as though Kings Cross were at Piccadilly Circus, or Bombay Terminus were on the waterfront. The only Terminus I know to be similarly placed is Central Station in New York ; that also is right there. Waverley Station lies deep down in the earth, with Edinburgh rising above on all sides. Climb the granite steps from the platform and one stands in Princes Street in all its glory. Edinburgh is entirely different from any other British City ; it is planned differently and built differently. It is incredibly beautiful and dignified, and its natural dignity and atmosphere is reflected right throughout the City and its inhabitants. It is reflected in what the people say and do ; in how they dress their shop windows ; in how one is received at one's hotel, and how one is served with a bus ticket. If anyone is ever rude or snappy to anyone else in Edinburgh I have yet to experience it. Stroll down the two miles of Princes Street, and note the quiet dignity and solid luxury

of the famous shops. Take coffee at Crawford's or Mackie's, and let yourself go on the long low cakes studded with almonds. Note the Banks and Clubs on Princes Street where one ascends steps to gain admittance, and the bookshops off Princes Street with similar steps, except that here one goes down to arrive at the shop door. American visitors will find Edinburgh strangely reminiscent of Philadelphia, with the streets at right angles and the crescents behind with their tall, solid, stone houses. Edinburgh Hotels must be classed as the best in the world. The North British, the Royal British and the Caledonia, to mention only three, receive their visitors with a courtesy and efficiency that, for the moment, seems to be dying out in many cities. One's first visit to Edinburgh is unforgettable, and one always yearns to return. Perhaps it is the soft voices and kind faces of its people, or the feeling of well being one experiences there. Perhaps one gains something from the history steeped atmosphere of the place that so obviously controls the behaviour of its people. Perhaps it is just because it is Scotland.

EDINBURGH

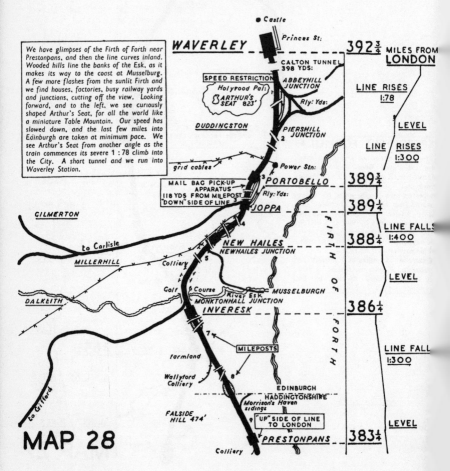

● Castle

WAVERLEY — — —   Princes St: 392¾ MILES FROM
                                                LONDON
                    CALTON TUNNEL
                    398 YDS:
SPEED RESTRICTION   ABBEYHILL   LINE RISES
Holyrood Pal: JUNCTION   1:78
ARTHUR'S
SEAT 823'   Rly: Yds:
                                               LEVEL
DUDDINGSTON
                    PIERSHILL   LINE   RISES
                    JUNCTION   1:300
                2
          grid cables   ● Power Stn:
                    PORTOBELLO   389¾
MAIL BAG PICK-UP   Rly: Yds:
APPARATUS
118 YDS FROM MILEPOST
DOWN SIDE OF LINE 3 JOPPA   389¼

GILMERTON   LINE FALLS
                                                1:400
                    NEW HAILES   388¼
to Carlisle   NEWHAILES JUNCTION
MILLERHILL   Colliery   5   LEVEL
                 6 Course
Golf   River Esk MUSSELBURGH
DALKEITH   MONKTONHALL JUNCTION
                    INVERESK   386¼

                7
                    MILEPOSTS   LINE FALL
                                                1:300
            farmland
        Wallyford
        Colliery   8
                         EDINBURGH
                    HADDINGTONSHIRE
                    Morrison's Haven
to Gifford   sidings
            FALSIDE   9 "UP" SIDE OF LINE
            HILL 474'   TO LONDON   LEVEL

MAP 28   PRESTONPANS   383¼
            Colliery

We have glimpses of the Firth of Forth near Prestonpans, and then the line curves inland. Wooded hills line the banks of the Esk, as it makes its way to the coast at Musselburg. A few more flashes from the sunlit Firth and we find houses, factories, busy railway yards and junctions, cutting off the view. Looking forward, and to the left, we see curiously shaped Arthur's Seat, for all the world like a miniature Table Mountain. Our speed has slowed down, and the last few miles into Edinburgh are taken at minimum pace. We see Arthur's Seat from another angle as the train commences its severe 1 : 78 climb into the City. A short tunnel and we run into Waverley Station.

FIRTH OF FORTH

SELL YOUR FIRST STORY THIS WINTER

PANEL OF AUTHORS & EDITORS FORM NEW POSTAL SCHOOL

APPLICATIONS are invited from men and women of all ages to enter the profession of authorship under the guidance of a panel of modern successful authors and editors formed to encourage and to direct new writers. All applicants must possess the urge to write and be prepared to devote at least a few hours of spare time a week to the successful new methods laid down by:—

7 SPECIALISTS ADVISE

1. Author of over 1,000 modern short stories.
2. Editor of one of the best-selling women's magazines.
3. A prolific writer of women's serials now actually appearing in the journals of one of the biggest periodical publishing houses of the world.
4. The writer of over a million words about Bessie Bunter.
5. A regular contributor to all the best-selling Juvenile periodicals.
6. Feature Editor of Sunday newspaper.
7. Sub-Editor of national daily.

The creative instinct is of all things in the most worthy of development and expression. There are many folk with the gift to see and record Life in the routine around them, with natures sensitive to the humour, pathos and excitement of their experience, who with correct guidance quickly could be expressing themselves in well-paid articles and stories and, perhaps, making for themselves a lasting name in the world of letters.

Influence and wealth—No help
Humble education—No bar

There is a lesson all would-be writers must learn. It has usually only been acquired after long, painful experience. Now it can be learned quickly by those able and willing to profit from the crystallised experience of successful writers.

The need for direction

There is to-day a great demand for good English fiction of all types. The shortage is so great that American fiction is invading the English markets. If ever there was an opportunity for the new writer and the writer who wishes to expand his field, it is here now.

The old methods of selling stories have changed. New publications and periodicals are springing up almost week by week. There is no reason why anyone with a gift for expression and a feeling for words cannot almost immediately learn to use that gift and be paid handsomely for doing so. All that so many writers lack is direction on how and where to start, how and where to finish and, above all, where to sell. No ordinary friend can help. Prejudiced criticisms are no use. The Fleet Street School of Authorship has been formed by authors who are writing in Fleet Street to-day. They have learnt their lesson from experience. They know that a man must eat as well as write, that he must earn while he is learning as indeed they did themselves.

A "Source" of Income

The new course is far more than a course of study. It would more properly be called a "course of Income." From the very earliest lessons it must be producing saleable work and actually introducing the writer to his market. It is the intention that the fees for the course shall be paid for by accepted contributions as far as possible and special arrangements are available for those of limited means whose ability justifies them "working their passage" to success.

How to Apply

All who feel they can be helped by this course, as described, and who feel their talent justifies the effort, are requested to apply for details of the new plan of writing to sell. Those who start now will have every opportunity to appear in print this winter, if they have the necessary drive and ambition. The book *The Prospects for Authorship* is sent under plain, sealed cover to all who apply. Application entails no obligation and it is particularly requested that no money be sent in this first instance. **Write now for the personal attention of the Director of Studies, Desk 11, The Fleet Street School of Authorship, 45 Chancery Lane, Fleet Street, London, W.C.2.** (Stamp for reply postage appreciated.)

'Good Mornings' begin with Gillette

Life and soul of the carriage, behold Mr. Gay who boasts that his blades make him bright for the day!

HOT **OXO**
so good to drink...
so easy to make

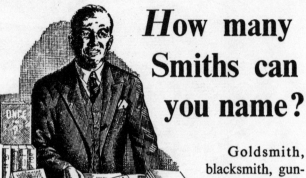

How many Smiths can you name?

Goldsmith, blacksmith, gunsmith, coppersmith, locksmith: ten to one, before your list is half-a-dozen long, you will think of the news, book and stationery "Smith." For the Smith who supplies your newspapers and magazines, the books you buy and the books you borrow, your stationery (and, on occasion, does your printing, your bookbinding and your advertising) is at your service at 1,500 bookshops and station bookstalls throughout England and Wales.

The W. H. Smith & Son bookshop or bookstall manager or assistant is a cheerful and deservedly popular personality; and if present-day supply problems have somewhat reduced the number and variety of his wares, so that he is sometimes unable to supply all your needs, he is nevertheless still the best source for those that are available.

W. H. SMITH & SON

1,500 BOOKSHOPS AND STATION BOOKSTALLS

Head Office: W. H. Smith & Son, Ltd., Strand House, W.C.2

This is the way to
RHEUMATIC RELIEF

'Curicones' have proved a turning point in the life of many a Rheumatic sufferer.
This great treatment has brought freedom from the cruel pains of Rheumatism,
Gout, Lumbago, Sciatica, Neuritis, Synovitis, Fibrositis, Swollen Joints, and
kindred ills.   The large volume of testimony, accumulated over years, is ample
tribute to the power of 'CURICONES.'   Such testimony cannot be denied.
**It is your assurance of the substantial relief that 'Curicones' have
brought to others.**   All ingredients in 'Curicones' are fully approved by the
British Pharmaceutical Authoritiies.   Begin a course of 'Curicones' today.

FROM ALL CHEMISTS

LIFE ASSURANCE IN ACTION

A MAN TOOK out a Prudential "Heritage Endowment." Six months later he died. His dependants receive £5 a week for over 15 years, and then a final payment of £2,750. In all £6,780 will be paid.

IF YOU TAKE out a present day "Heritage Endowment" policy for £2,000 there will be

FOR YOURSELF

if you live 20 years

£2,000 with Bonuses added.

FOR YOUR FAMILY

Should you die within 20 years,

£200 CASH at death together with Bonuses.

£6 A WEEK for the remainder of the 20 years, and

£1,800 CASH at the end of 20 years from the date of the Policy.

Fill in and forward this Coupon

To **THE PRUDENTIAL ASSURANCE CO. L** Holborn Bars, London, E.C.1

I desire full particulars of your "Heritage Endowment" Policy.

Name .... Date of Birth ....

Address ....

T.O.R. 1946 ....

P.P.522